AF583116

From Mine.... .

To Yours.... .

Ms. Tarannum Dhange is a multifaceted individual whose life journey seamlessly blends creativity, intellect, and entrepreneurship. A Civil Engineer with an MBA in Finance, she is a visionary business owner who successfully operated a chain of cafes in Mumbai.

Beyond her professional accomplishments, Ms. Dhange is a fitness enthusiast, participates in marathons and is a passionate poet whose heartfelt expressions resonate deeply with readers. Her debut poetry collection, My Soul, My Life, offers a poignant exploration of love, loss, resilience, and self-discovery. Each poem reflects her ability to capture the essence of emotions and transform them into lyrical masterpieces that inspire introspection.

With a natural flair for storytelling, Ms. Dhange invites readers on a reflective journey through the complexities of relationships, the depth of human experiences, and the power of personal growth. Her unique perspective, shaped by her diverse career and life experiences, shines through in every verse, making her work relatable and profoundly moving.

Through her poems, Ms. Dhange aspires to connect with her readers on a soul level, offering them a source of solace and inspiration. Her words are not merely poems but an invitation to celebrate the beauty and intricacies of life itself.

From Mine... to Yours... would not be complete without expressing my heartfelt gratitude to the one who has been the driving force behind its creation.

These emotions, etched within these pages, are dedicated to the most special people in my life—those who have promised to stand by me, no matter where life's journey leads us. To my Mom and Dad, whose love and guidance have been my foundation; my partner, Majid, for being my unwavering support; my shining star, Aayan, who brings light to my days; and Tabassum, Mohammed, and little Zain, who fill my life with joy and meaning.

To my family, both near and far, and to my friends who have always encouraged me to reach for my dreams—your belief in me has been a source of immense strength.

Finally, to everyone who has played a part in bringing this journey into existence, I extend my deepest gratitude. This book is as much yours as it is mine.

Tarannum .

To Aayan

FROM MINE..... TO YOURS.....

The soul has its own life - a journey that found a way from mine to yours.

From Mine to Yours is a collection of poems; it is a reflection of a journey through the vast and intricate landscapes of emotion and thought.

Love is expressed in various forms and life is expressed as the voyage transcending time and space. When the walk starts in search of a friend, it goes through the myriad stages of relationships and emotions -a path which paves way for a life which is shared between mine and yours.

Each poem is a snapshot of time, an invitation to feel, to reflect and to connect with the rawness of shared human experience, drawing us closer to understanding one another and ourselves.

It is an expression and a hope to offer a sense of presence- a reminder to simply just be. Even when lost, perhaps these words will find its path within through thoughts and moments shared.

Welcome to the journey together.

From Mine..... To Yours.....

PREFACE

From Mine To Yours holds a special place in my heart, as it has served as a bridge connecting the essence of My Soul, My Life.

As I poured my thoughts onto the page in various forms, each moment carried its own significance, painted with the emotions of life's ever-changing seasons. These moments are reflected in the vibrant hues that life brings along its journey.

As an author who has found solace in these words, I hope they bring a splash of colour to your heart and awaken flashes of memory as you sail through the sea of emotions they carry.

This book is not just a compilation of written pieces; it is a tapestry of feelings - love, loss, hope, and discovery- moments of vulnerability and strength that I've woven together.

A part of me somewhere in you where it is etched finitely infinite.

From Mine..... To Yours.....

FROM MINE..... TO YOURS.....

Friendship

A relation that needs no boundaries,
A face that needs no name,
Endless are the emotions,
Bound by the threads of love,
As you walk the path of life.

A friend is a soul so dear,
A heart that beats in another soul,
A soul that feels another heart.

A being who gives you strength in your weakness,
A light which gives direction to your path,
A guide who enlightens your actions,
A strength in your descend.

Emotions don't require verdict,
Words don't articulate,
Thoughts are not bound by ambits,
There's no fracas in hearts.
There's no aversion of feelings.

The souls so pure,
The minds pristine,
Such is the magic of friendship,
Such is the grace of the word.

Bound by the thread of love,
A relation that needs no epithet.
A feeling that needs no closure.

My Soul, My Life is,
From Mine To Yours.

From Mine..... To Yours..... .

Relations in essence

The rhythm in the womb, is the heart of a mother.
The finger that holds, is the warmth of a father.
The feet that run, is the pride of a grandparent.
The caress of love is the care for the progeny.

As a child grows,

He has relations to share, he has emotions to bare.
Friends soon fill the gap and who once knew your day, awaits, although you are just some numbers away.
Relations change like the seasons of the year,
Who cares if you choose to differ.

Remember the clock ticking,

Has a cycle to ride,
Time is always not going to be your tide.
Today you can sail the rough seas,
Tomorrow the eyes will search the highs.

We all have the loved ones who care,
We all have various relations to share.

Do not falter on the path you travel,
Carry it all along this journey of Life,
Let not time falter, essence of each time.
Walk back on the path you travelled,
You will find imprints of each you dwelled.
Smile that your mirror reflects its memories,
Cherish that your heart reminisces its substance.

You will have your love to nurture.
There is always someone waiting at the distance,
You will have to travel to reach up to that destination.

Do not leave the love incomplete,
It has its forms for you to reach.
Walk with the warmth that felt first,
Hold with the fervour that fondled first.

Love has its forms; Relations has its name.
Let it smile with pride; let it leave with smile.

Relations, always begin to never end,
Relations, always live to never die.
Let them be existent, Let them be essence.

The Language of Love.

A feeling of oneness of the hearts that beat,
A gesture of happiness of the moments that live,
An ache of the sadness of the hurt that feels,
A smile of happiness of the triumph that eyes see.

Pure as it is,
It doesn't require words to express the vexation,
It doesn't want actions to express the fervour,
Silence is its language and tears are the solace,
Tolerance is its endearment and smile is the soothe.

When silence takes over words, its slits its essence,
When actions take over expressions, it shatters the yearn,
Words create a fracas of thoughts, to the divinity of souls,
Actions leave a scar, to the purity of heart.

Let not life falter its faith,
Let not love to unpen its worth,
Let not relations be influence by the world,
Let not divinity be contingent of circumstances.

Let even anger be astonished in its conduct,
Let even love reach the horizon only to reflect,
Let even divinity sink in the depths of the ocean only to rise,
Let even love rise and shine with the sun only to be seen in
the night as stars in the sky.
Let not the essence within ever detach for love to be etched
within our souls.

From Mine..... To Yours..... .

Emotions

Silent eyes express feelings that words cannot express,
No matter how hard one tries, it's impossible to win against loved ones.
As I endured every moment that someone else graced in,
When life returned to me, I learned to embrace it with a smile.

There was something missing in life, like an empty void,
I searched for completeness in the feeling of love.
I saw a boat drifting away from the shore,
I sought support from the tiniest straws.
When life scattered across the world,
I learned to gather those fragmented moments into a whole.

Your presence feels like a part of destiny,
As if life was separated only to unite.

Your every word settles in my mind in such a way,
As thoughts inked together in my life.
Moments spent with you nestle deep in my heart,
Like dreams that closed eyes see.
Your feelings touch my soul in a way,
Like raindrops moistening the earth every day.

Your presence in my life feels like a dream,
I fear it doesn't open too soon,
Dreams seen by awakened eyes shatter too soon.

My heartbeat is enthralled to your smile,
A life without you feels incomplete.

The roads may lead us further apart,
But let's not lose each other amidst changing paths.

This life of mine, though small, is a shadow walking your path.
May we complete the final journey of life together.
Let my feeling stay with you like this,
As though every breath remains connected to life
Until they breathe their last.

From Mine.... . To Yours.... .

Longing

Days go by when the eyes wait to smile,
Time stands still the distance seems to grow,
Heart cheers the loneliness, that lies within,
Moments sparkle the emptiness under.

The love we share doesn't require acceptance,
It bestows understanding.
The silence doesn't require judgement,
It realises its actions.
The lips don't need to express,
It smiles in euphoria.
The eyes don't need to shy,
It gleams in its yearning.

We may be not too close in distance,
But we are not too far along the path,
We may not be together tangibly,
But we are not distant from the souls,
We may not sojourn in presence,
But love is all along in the journey.

Loneliness may tiptoe the mind,
But rhythm will fill the heart,
Thoughts may claim control,
But memories will embrace the parting.

Life may move on, heart will hang on,
To the moments incomplete,
To the chimera of life,
To the fondle of love,
To the summit of souls.

Love is a journey, we meet there somewhere,
Love is a feeling, we live within it everywhere,
Love is us; we will always be there.

From Mine.... . To Yours.... .

Day seems longer, Night doesn't travel.
It seems a decade of silence,
It seems the heart yearns your touch.
Your thoughts traverse my path,
Your words replicate in my actions.

The moments spend together, are the solace of my day,
The linings in the sky are the hope of my night,
There is emptiness in my existence,
There is gloom in the distance.

But,
The distance doesn't seem to detach our souls,
The exclusion doesn't seem to diminish our love,
The absence doesn't seem to muffle our feelings,
The loneliness doesn't seem to detach our existence.

Await,
Till the aurora hits the sky to brighten our mornings,
Till the heart rings in happiness to the warble of the song,
Till the soul melts in ardour of the dusk to climax.

Let the fervour of love power our emotions,
Let the tranquillity of soul steer our paths,
Let distance be the course for resolve of our love,
Let infinity find its way, in this finite little world.

From Mine..... To Yours..... .

Together in Solitude

When my silence is heard, I feel togetherness,
When in loneliness you hold, I feel togetherness,
When the tear doesn't roll down my cheek, I feel togetherness,
When that little giggle makes it all, I feel togetherness.

I may be ready to walk the path alone, but maybe you need to be the shadow,
I may be able to fight that darkness within, but maybe you need to be the gleam,
I may be able to carry that silence, but maybe you need to hear,
I may be doing it all alone, but maybe you need to hold on.

Maybe love can have expressions abundant, but sometimes it needs to be perceived,
Maybe loneliness can be dealt with warmth, but assertion in gesture is to be noticed,
Maybe absence can be handled with patience, but sometimes the touch is to be entailed,
Maybe the heart can brawl with the mind in silence, but the madness needs to be admirable.

Be my strength in your absence,
Be my thoughts in your silence,
Be my touch in your distance,
Be present even in your absence.

Be together even when alone.
Be there even when gone.

For divinity to exist,
For infinity till it's finite.

From Mine.... . To Yours.... .

Boundaries

Your presence in my life hasn't come with wants,
Your absence in it won't dwindle your essence,
There were no fringes when it came to the bond,
There were no extremities finite.

When relations cast about desires,
When the souls deviate of its resolve,
There is chasm in warmth,
There is desolation profound.

Let We not set boundaries obscure,
Let We not vamoose sketchy,
Let the world cherish if they know,
Let the thoughts delight within.

For there are relations with boundaries,
Let us make We that strikes the heart,
Let us make We that bonds the purpose.

Whatever we be, wherever we see,
Boundaries be the horizon,
Of a relation finite,
Until the smile attains finitely infinite.

From Mine.... . To Yours.... .

Tears

As a drop it rolls down my cheek,
As a smile it whispers on my lips,
As a moment it sinks in my heart,
As fire it rushes in my blood.

It is a fervour which my heart holds,
It is a reflection which my soul sees,
It is an odyssey which life flourishes,
It is a diction of my thoughts.

Let it be a paradigm of my feelings,
Let it recess in your heart like my love,
Let it clash like the splice of our words,
Let it behold like the essence of my silence.

Let the tears cry, Let the tears voice.
Let the throb reach, Let my eyes speak.

From Mine.... . To Yours.... .

When Life happens, it comes with its own challenges.
What we yearn is what we are tested for,
What we have in abundance is marked for its handle.
What is gifted is asked to be portioned out.

When you are born your journey to enlighten begins,
A bird learns to leave the nest, that's sacrifice.
A child learns to walk alone, that's sacrifice.
A lover learns to unhand, that's sacrifice.
A partner learns to empathise, that's sacrifice.
A parent learns to relinquish, that's sacrifice.
When you die your soul departs, that's sacrifice.

Sacrifice to be anchored to your thoughts,
Sacrifice if it tranquils your soul,
Sacrifice if it cherishes your heart,
Sacrifice because a night will end for the sun to rise.
Sacrifice because a heart has healed, for a life to revive.

From Mine.... . To Yours.... .

Silence

The words echoed its thoughts in silence,
As the heart throb its rhythm,
As the mind swerved its path,
Feelings chase the trail of moments,
As time ceases to walk.

The night seems lingering,
The day seems astray,
The moments scattered,
The faith gravitates.

The path we walk seems arduous,
But the credence of essence prevails.
The warmth we share may tumult,
But the touch of fervour lingers.
The touch we sense seems complex,
But the soul that discerns divine.

Silence cannot astray our thoughts,
Distance cannot detach our warmth,
Words can disappear,
Vison can dissipate,
Thoughts cannot be perished,
Love can never be assessed,
Life can never be silenced.

From Mine..... To Yours.....

Forgiveness

When I recollect the path less travelled,
My anger silences within.
When I reminisce the moments we shared,
My lips sparkle.
When I ponder on the words that flowed,
My thoughts drift.

There were junctures in the journey,
Where we fragmented only to behold.
There was cadence in the speech,
When we squabbled only to assent.
There was a slash of hearts,
When we evaded our own warmth only to unify.

Time has tranquil the pain within,
Healed is the aridity of my soul,
The vacuum is filled with solace of love,
The intensity of accord has dwindled with time,
Forgiven is my soul, for life to sojourn.

You will find me there, where you never delved into.

From Mine.... . To Yours.... .

Memories

The countless breaths I took when we were together are my memories,
The moments when we held each other are framed in my heart,
The words that you wrote when you missed me are rooted deep,
The voice that echoed my name is etched on my soul.

Countless moments of that smile will never fade,
That mornings when I woke with your breathe,
That touch which I felt when the stars were dancing in paradise,
That warmth that held the soul in fervour,
The care which expressed when tears rolled down,
The love that showered like the rain from the sky.

Moments created; Memories etched.

When I look in the mirror, it reflects you,
When I close my eyes, it feels the kiss,
When I hold my hands, it feels the touch,
When I smile in loneliness, it feels you.

That every little thing I did in that moment was for you,
That smile I worn for you to behold,
That shine on my face for you to remember,
That path we walked when we held our hand,
That dance we swayed in our arms to fall,
That every second of it, for us was it all.

Memories etched; Life lived.
For Souls to unite, For Love divine.

In heavens we meet,
Where divinity prevails.
Where souls unite,
In between existence and desire.

From Mine..... To Yours..... .

The journey started alone, paths kept crossing,
Bright were my mornings; nights awakened my soul.

Pure as a star, my heart worn its shine,
Trust was the pillar; belief was the resolve.
Wandering among the rights and wrongs of life,
The path was long, faith walked it alone.

The desire to find myself never ceased,
The soul was blemished of its own credence,
The heart sank in its own abstract,
Life still yearned of its own thoughts.

Deep as I walked in this darkness of life,
A ray smiled at my eyes to confide,
Faith shined in the sun, for the belief it longed.

I found you there, where the horizon was met,
Heart sank in hope, fear seized the soul,
Resolve wanted to embrace, desire warned within,
I walked the path once again; faith now isn't ready to walk alone.
Soul still wishes that touch; Heart still awaits that hold.

Friendship is like the stars in the sky,
It exists even when the sun shines bright,
It twinkles even when the moon spreads its light.

Love is like the dawn and the dusk of the heart,
It will rise and fall never to depart.

Behold the journey, we have paths to cross,
Let me exist, for belief profound,
Let me be felt, for resolve sound.

Unspoken thoughts, Unheard feelings,
Your touch heals my heart, soul awaits its essence.
You hold me there where eyes don't see,
You feel me then, within I sink in.

The journey started alone,
Our paths crossed, only to behold,
The journey not to end alone.

The chaos has silenced my words,
It still speaks its heart,
The distance has fracas of thoughts,
It still longs to be realised.

Unaware if it reaches where the heart yearned,
Adrift the soul stands still.
Let relation not silence, Let life not fail.

Let us we be, Let it just be.
From eternity, To infinity.

From Mine..... To Yours..... .

Hope

In the rising of the sun, I have you,
In the dusk that falls upon, I feel you,
Your warmth is there, when I want to hold you,
Your touch is there, when I want to feel you,
Whenever I close my eyes, you smile in peace,
Whenever I wake up bright, you smile in peace.

You speak a thousand words with my silence,
You love a thousand times in my loneliness,
You are there even in absence,
You are there even when non-existent.

Hope is,
To see another day with you,
To smile another night with you,
To love one more time with you,
To live one more life with you.
To have everything together with you.

From Mine..... To Yours..... .

Oneness

Even if thoughts don't match, disagreement doesn't sink in,
Even when ideologies differ, purpose doesn't hamper,
Even when words oppose, ideas matter.
Even when actions can be rebellious, expressions find their connect.

I feel oneness.

There is difference in articulation, but love is in its language,
There may be err in judgement, but belief is in its path,
There is opinion specified, but criticism doesn't breathe,
There is idea that deliberates, methods may find an ear.

I feel oneness.

Never let the perception die,
Never let the retribution overpower,
Never let the dialogue quarrel,
Never let the arrogance survive.

I will still feel oneness.

Even if distance ever sinks in,

My silence will shadow the outrage,
My actions will leave you pondering,
My words will chaperone your deeds,
My smile will make it going.

I will still live in oneness.
I will still love our oneness.

From Mine.... . To Yours.... .

Lost but Found

It was as if the sun was about to rise but darkness withheld itself.
Inexorable as it felt, the clouds refused to smile.
There was fire in the brightness, stars sheltered beneath.

Love had its resolve; it chose to relinquish.
Silence was the mind, turmoil as it felt,
For the life gone by, forgotten was the feat.
As the dew fell upon, the moments healed itself.
As the world moved on, life stood still.

When I needed to be held, you walked the path alone,
When I needed an ear, you choose to brush my thoughts.
When there was loneliness, engrossed were you in your world.

When I needed that friend, astray was that hand.
When my soul sobbed within, it didn't reach your heart.

Now,
The tears don't roll,
The heart doesn't sadden,
The soul lives in silence,
The love denies to exist.

Still,
Love had its resolve; it chose to relinquish.
Stars shine above, only to coexist.
The cloud seems to be still; it still carries the weight.
The dawn awaits the dusk, as twilight unfolds.
Let it reach your heart; let it touch your soul.

From Mine.... To Yours.... .

In the darkest of my nights, I found hope,
When I was under the sod, you stimulated life.
The dots were buried within, you were the solace,
When I chose to preclude, you shepherd my path.

We never bound ourselves of the paths we walk,
We give credence to thoughts that are ours,
We sculpt our souls with Love that's divine,
We trace our Lives with the cord of rhythm.

There may be times when notions clash,
There may be lines which will contrast,
We may pass the destination one reached,
You look down and find the imprints of each.

When we reach the horizon,
Remember to look back and scrabble around,
There will be Life reloaded,
There will be evocation profound.
It shall be We and We just let it be.

From Mine..... To Yours..... .

Sentience

When I see you, my eyes gleam in warmth.
When I hear you, the melody of your voice echoes.
When I touch you, you leave a trace on my heart.
My love, you make me feel myself.

Your presence makes life exist,
Your thoughts make love fulfil,
Your words calm my soul,
Your feel fondles my heart.
My love, you make me feel myself.

When the sun rises, your wishes brighten my day,
When dusk falls upon, your love fills my sky.
When the rhythm of my heart, touches upon your soul,
My love, you make me feel myself.

When it rains, it showers upon in fragrance.
When seasons change, it brings in new desires.
When paths cross, memories usher.
When life will end, love remains ingrained.
My love, you make me feel myself.

Witness our love with our eyes,
Discern our sentiments with our touch,
Let silence speak in tenderness,
Let emotions take over fracas.

My love makes us feel complete.

From Mine..... To Yours..... .

Within

When I see you, my eyes gleam in warmth.
When I hear you, the melody of your voice echoes.
When I touch you, you leave a trace on my heart.
My love you make me feel myself.

Your presence makes life exist,
Your thoughts make love fulfil,
Your words calm my soul,
Your feel fondles my heart.
My love you make me feel myself.

When the sun rises, your wishes brighten my day,
When dusk falls upon, your love fills my sky.
When the rhythm of my heart, touches upon your soul,
My love you make me feel myself.

When it rains, it showers upon in fragrance.
When seasons change, it brings in new desires.
When paths cross, memories usher.
When life will end, love remains ingrained.
My love you make me feel myself.

Witness our love with our eyes,
Discern our sentiments with our touch,
Let silence speak in tenderness,
Let emotions take over fracas.

My love makes us feel complete.

From Mine.... . To Yours.... .

A Journey to Forever

Heal the hearts, with the fondness of our thoughts,
Forgive along the path, proffer yourself with virtue,
Be cognizant of your bustle, let cadence measure your thoughts.

The boat must reach the oasis of love,
The sail must achieve the fervour,
The paths we walk must shadow our hearts,
The conclude of the road must advance together.

When the destination is reached, the walk should seem worthy,
When the memories usher, the eyes should sparkle,
When the wind fondles, the touch should discern.
When the music follows, the rhythm should revive.

Let our love never diminish,
Let our souls never fragment,
Let our words never falter,
Let the essence never fail,
Let it always sphere within.

From Mine..... To Yours..... .

A Milestone

When you first walked, I felt life ran,
When you first spoke, I felt life whispered,
When you first wrote I felt life sang.

A ladder we were together to climb,
A step closer we were to reaching each time,
We faltered, We stumbled.
We rose, We endured.
Life spiralled around.

Today as you reach the last step of ladder,
The journey remains, the path is yet to attain.

Remember,
You have rivers to cross,
You have mountains to scale.

As you walk the path today,
My fingers still holding onto you,
My eyes still shielding for you,
The distance has diminished,
But the walk is arduous.

So, behold with courage and faith,
And walk with candour and belief,
Life has lessons to accord,
Time has merit to resolve.

You are My Soul, You are My Life.
As it flows,
From Mine To Yours.
To Reach,
From Soul, To Heart.

From Mine.... . To Yours.... .

www.ingramcontent.com/pod-product-compliance
Lightning Source LLC
LaVergne TN
LVHW021342160826
845679LV00008B/1451

* 9 7 9 8 8 9 6 3 2 8 5 1 3 *